**Roberto Cui**

# Oil Multinationals in Nigeria

## Human Rights, Sustainable Development and the Law

Anchor Academic
Publishing

**Cui, Roberto: Oil Multinationals in Nigeria: Human Rights, Sustainable Development and the Law, Hamburg, Anchor Academic Publishing 2015**

Buch-ISBN: 978-3-95489-369-0
PDF-eBook-ISBN: 978-3-95489-869-5
Druck/Herstellung: Anchor Academic Publishing, Hamburg, 2015

**Bibliografische Information der Deutschen Nationalbibliothek:**
Die Deutsche Nationalbibliothek verzeichnet diese Publikation in der Deutschen
Nationalbibliografie; detaillierte bibliografische Daten sind im Internet über
http://dnb.d-nb.de abrufbar.

**Bibliographical Information of the German National Library:**
The German National Library lists this publication in the German National Bibliography.
Detailed bibliographic data can be found at: http://dnb.d-nb.de

© Anchor Academic Publishing, Imprint der Diplomica Verlag GmbH
Hermannstal 119k, 22119 Hamburg
http://www.diplomica-verlag.de, Hamburg 2015
Printed in Germany

*For those who suffer.*


*Once it has started, rot is hard to stop, whether in a body or a nation.*

PETER MAASS, *Crude World: The Violent Twilight of Oil.*

*Abstract*

*Decades of irresponsible oil exploitation in the Niger Delta have caused a water and air pollution which does not have many comparisons anywhere else. In an already fragile country as Nigeria, characterised by weak democratic institutions and poor economic governance, this situation has led to increasing discontent and violence towards both the government and the oil multinationals. These two actors co-operate for the maximisation of oil profits and revenues while, at the same time, excluding local host communities from the participation in oil development projects, preventing them from achieving a sustainable development, violating their human rights, and compromising their livelihoods.*

*This book analyses the Nigerian legal framework in the oil sector and the peculiarities of the country in order to provide a critical overview of the issues, demonstrating that the amendment of the domestic Acts dealing with the topic, as well as the remediation to the damages caused by the oil multinationals, are no longer deferrable. The final aim is to suggest a pattern to sustainable oil development that, by means of applying the concepts of Corporate Social Responsibility, would help to quell the conflict, to improve local people's standards of life, and to make Nigeria emerge as a socio-environmentally responsible African resource-rich country.*

# Table of Contents

# Introduction

The starting point of this work lies in the need of deepening the study on the Nigerian oil sector, as one of the world most astonishing examples of mismanagement of energy resources.

Therefore, the research will be carried out with the aim of enlightening an aspect of energy which is often omitted in the mainstream academic and institutional panorama of developed countries.

Indeed, while the European Union and its member states, as well as the United States, are increasingly stressing the importance of environment protection and sustainability in energy development projects,[1] many major multinational corporations (MNCs) based in the EU and in the US, are still heavily involved in the pollution of those developing countries which are not able nor willing to regulate their own energy sector in such a way to avoid harmful social and environmental consequences. Nigeria – a country where religious and ethnical separation and socio-political contradictions are embedded in the daily life since the independence from Britain – is a typical example of this kind of situation.

Hence, the study will seek to clarify the problem of irresponsible exploitation of oil resources in a country which does not have a proper legislative framework dealing with the topic while, at the same time, protecting their citizens' rights.

---

[1] As a way of example, see: European Commission, 'Sustainable, secure and affordable energy for Europeans' (europa.eu 2013). Available at: <http://europa.eu/pol/ener/flipbook/en/files/energy.pdf> accessed on 15 August 2014, and
The Business Council for Sustainable Energy, 'Sustainable energy in America. Fact-book 2014' (bcse.org 2014). Available at:
<http://www.bcse.org/factbook/pdfs/2014%20Sustainable%20Energy%20in%20America%20Factbook. pdf> accessed on 15 August 2014.

Oil activities in Nigeria began in the mid 1950s; nowadays the country is the fifth exporter of crude oil, and the twelfth as regards crude oil production, despite the fact that its oil consumption level is far less significant.[2]

The research will take into particular consideration the role of oil multinational corporations[3] in a three-fold relationship: MNCs and environment; MNCs and local communities; MNCs and central government. These three elements will represent the common thread across the entire study.

The vast national legal framework in the oil sector does not set a protection for the communities and territories affected by the petroleum exploration and industrial activities, leading to a situation in which the uneven allocation of land rights and distribution of wealth causes conflict, environmental degradation and human and peoples' rights violations.

The aim of the research is, firstly, to provide a deep account of the Nigerian legal framework related to oil, in order to highlight the contradictions and lacunas that led to the current situation; secondly, to link this analysis to the study of ethnicity, society and environment in the country; thirdly, to match these features with Corporate Social Responsibility, seeking to incorporate its concepts to the national body of rules, in the view of the achievement of sustainability in the development of such a controversial energy resource.

Accordingly, Chapter 1 carries out the critical analysis of the Nigerian legal framework in the oil sector; Chapter 2 explores the peculiar social and

---

[2] CIA, 'The World Fact-book Nigeria' (cia.gov 2014). Available at:
<https://www.cia.gov/library/publications/the-world-factbook/geos/ni.html> accessed on 25 July 2014.
[3] The debate about the difference between Multinational Corporations and Transnational Corporations originated during the early discussion on international enterprises having their headquarters in one country but carrying out business in various parts of the world. Here, this difference is not relevant: for the purposes of this work, Transnational Corporations and Multinational Corporations are regarded as the same kind of international business.

environmental asset of the country, in order to demonstrate the need of a revision of the legislative framework; Chapter 3 proposes recommendations on the possible avenues which can eventually be followed by Nigeria; Chapter 4 concludes.

The innovative contribution of the study lies in its approach, and, in particular, in the attempt of drawing a scheme by which every element involved in the oil management would work together and help each other for the improvement of the environmental and social situation and the achievement of a sustainable oil development pattern.

Federal government, local governments and communities, and MNCs shall assume their own share of responsibility in this process.

# 1. The Nigerian legal regulation of the oil industry

This chapter will focus on the analysis of the main Nigerian Acts relating to the oil sector. The aim is to offer a critical overview of the legislative and regulatory framework in the country. Beside the national law, attention will be also paid to the international law instruments on human rights and environmental issues, as well as related to the control of multinational enterprises: oil exploration and production affect the environment in the Niger Delta and the livelihoods of the resident communities, which is tantamount to a violation of human rights.

The significance of studying the legal scheme lies in the fact that, as regards developing countries and especially Nigeria, the reasons behind the harmful consequences of a major industry's activities (like oil development) can be found, first of all, exactly in the contradictions and loopholes of domestic Acts and Regulations. As a result, a better understanding of the law will help in considering how CSR can improve the legal standards and not only be regulated by them.

## 1. 1. National legislation

### 1.1.1. The Land Use Act (LUA) 1978

The Land Use Act (LUA) is the pillar of the Nigerian legal structure related to the management of land. It has a remarkable impact in the regulation of oil activities, given the characteristics of this sector.

Emerging from the scrutiny of the LUA, it is possible to say that it systemically transfers the land rights from the local communities and state governments to the federal state: this has led to a situation in which oil multinationals take advantage of the national low standards in the field of compensation, thus avoiding to comply with the standards set at the international level.

To be more precise, the reference, here, is to Section 28, which states that land may be appropriated from the federal State for "overriding public interest", and provides that the central government can require the land "for mining purposes and oil pipelines or for any purpose connected therewith."

Ako[4] demonstrates how the historical evolution of the Nigerian nation has led to a subtraction of land's rights from those communities who were traditionally entitled of the ownership and use of the lands and resources, by the federal government. According to the author, vesting all rights to lands and natural resources in the government is equivalent to a subtraction of the communities' environmental rights. As also argued by Atsegbua, indeed: "the denial of the existence of environmental rights is primarily responsible for the under-development of the Niger Delta area."[5]

The 2003 WAC Global Services Report, entitled "Peace and Security in the Niger Delta", recognises that the main cause of conflict is not represented by the corporate policies, but by the actual practices. Nonetheless, the same report also

---

[4] R T Ako, 'Nigeria's Land Use Act: an antithesis to environmental justice', [2009], JAL 53:2 289-304.
[5] L Atsegbua, 'Environmental rights, pipeline vandalisation and conflict resolution in Nigeria', [2001] IELTR 5 89-92.

states that "aspects of current policies (land acquisition, oil spill compensation, hiring and contracting) may feed into, or *even create conflict.*"[6] (Emphasis added).

The subtraction of the land from the local communities to the benefit of the oil sector constitutes one of the main reasons at the basis of the Nigerian environmental disaster, as well as the main cause of discontent and instability in the Niger Delta region.

The main outcome of the above discussion is that, although the MNCs claim their compliance to the law,[7] this is not sufficient to identify corporate good practices, based on justice and equity grounds.

*1.1.2. The Oil Pipelines Act (OPA) 1956 and the Petroleum (Drilling and Production) Regulations 1969*

Beside the misappropriation of rights to land and resources, it is appropriate to consider the compensation problem. The domestic Nigerian law is set in order to avoid the payment of fair and adequate compensation for the losses deriving from oil activities, both related to land acquisition and to environmental pollution.

When analysing the Nigerian legal framework in the oil sector, it could often appear that the provisions concerning this particular issue are clear enough to solve any dispute arising from eventual pipelines leakage or from any hazardous activity related to the oil industry.

In particular, Section 11(5) of the Oil Pipelines Act prescribes:

---

[6] Nyheim, Zandviliet, Morissey, 'Peace and Security in the Niger Delta: Conflict Expert Group Baseline Report,' (npr 2003) <http://www.npr.org/documents/2005/aug/shell_wac_report.pdf> accessed on 12 February 2014.
[7] See, for instance: Shell, 'Politically sensitive regions' (shell.com). Available at: <http://www.shell.com/global/environment-society/society/business/politically-sensitive-regions.html> accessed on 16 August 2014.

"The holder of a licence shall pay compensation to any person whose land or interest in land [...] is injuriously affected by the exercise of the rights conferred by the licence [...]; and to any person suffering damage by reason of any neglect on the part of the holder or his agents, servants or workmen to protect, maintain or repair any work structure or thing executed under the licence [...]; and to any person suffering for any damage (other than on account of his own default or on account of the malicious act of a third person) as a consequence of any breakage of or leakage from the pipeline or an ancillary installation."

However, the actual practices regarding compensation work in the opposite direction, since it is not always easy to achieve the agreement on the compensation amount, which is required by the OPA in order to avoid the issue to be brought to court.[8]

Sections 21(2) and 23 of the Petroleum (Drilling and Production) Regulations 1969 – set in accordance with the Petroleum Act 1956 – contemplate the payment of "fair and adequate compensation", respectively to the owners of economic trees in the event that these are cut or taken off for oil development purposes, and to fishermen, if the owner of a license *unreasonably* interferes with the exercise of their fishing rights.

As argued by various authors,[9] the legal framework on compensation represents an easy viable avenue for oil companies who want to escape liability for harmful consequences arising from oil activities.

---

[8] The last line of Section 11(5)(c) of OPA states: "If the amount of such compensation is not agreed between any such person and the holder, it shall be fixed by a court [...]."
[9] E.g. K S A Ebeku, 'Compensation for damage arising from oil operations: Shell Petroleum Development Company of Nigeria v Ambah revisited' [2002] IELTR 155, 156,
J G Frynas, *Oil in Nigeria, Conflict and Litigation between Oil Companies and Village Communities*. LIT, London 2000, and
O Adewale, 'Oil Spill Compensation Claims in Nigeria: Principles, Guidelines and Criteria' [1989] JAL, 33, 91-104.

According to Ebeku, the *onus probandi*, placed by Sections 21(2) and 23, on farmers and/or fishermen who actually suffer from these damages, turns to appear overwhelming for the claimants: this is an avenue through which "an oil operator [might] escape liability."[10]

Ebeku concludes that the wording of this provision "virtually robs the statute of its substance".[11]

Frynas maintains that "[in] Nigeria, oil companies have often alleged that damage from oil operations is due to sabotage, which is considered an act of a stranger."[12] The strategy adopted by the multinational companies operating in the country and sued for oil pollution consists in rebutting charges by claiming that the spills were caused "by the malicious act of third persons." Multinationals are allowed to do so by the already mentioned Section 11(5)(c) of the OPA, that obliges oil operators to pay compensation for damage resulting from oil spills, unless it occurred on "account of [the suffering person's] own default or [...] the malicious act of a third person." This provision, if not amended, deprives the clause contained in the Environmental Guidelines and Standards for the Petroleum Industry in Nigeria (EGASPIN) – according to which "operators incur responsibility for the containment and recovery for any spill discovered in their area, *whether or not its source is known*"[13] – of its significance.

---

[10] K S A Ebeku, supra note 9, p. 156.
[11] Ibid.
[12] J G Frynas, supra note 9, p. 196.
[13] Department of Petroleum of the Federal Republic of Nigeria, Environmental Guidelines and Standards for the Petroleum Industry in Nigeria, S 4.1. Emphasis added.

The Guidelines state that MNCs have the duty to implement actions to remedy to the oil spillage no matter the cause. But, they are no more than soft law, and, as such, not enforceable.

Hence, the liability for damages, arising from oil operations, and, as a consequence, the obligation to pay compensation, according to the Nigerian domestic framework, is not strict – being the claimant "required to prove negligence on the part of the operator."[14]

If the common corporate practice, consisting in avoiding negotiation and mediation in order to set the disputes against local claimants in courts or in arbitral tribunals,[15] is also taken into account, it is possible to argue that the burden of proof pending on the plaintiffs is actually unbearable.

Local communities and people's interests are not taken into account in the decision to use their land to the purpose of devoting it to oil development, nor in the phase of compensation for eventual harmful consequences arising from oil operations (by means of mediation and negotiation between MNCs and communities themselves): the want of commitment by MNCs to make the local communities participate in the development of their own territory can be regarded as a want of corporate best practices.

*1.1.3. The Companies and Allied Matters Act (CAMA) 1990*

The establishment of parent companies' liability for damages arising from their local subsidiaries' activity is another challenging aspect. Various observers and

---

[14] O Adewale, supra note 9, p. 95.
[15] K S A Ebeku, supra note 9, p. 155.

commentators have highlighted the fact that oil MNCs in Nigeria take advantage of the combination of bad practices and loose legal and regulatory framework.

Section 54(1) of the CAMA represents a crucial provision in the view of the attribution of liability to MNCs operating in Nigeria. According to it, "[...] every foreign company [...] incorporated outside Nigeria, and having the intention of carrying on business in Nigeria shall take all steps necessary to obtain incorporation as a separate entity in Nigeria for that purpose [...]."

*Prima facie*, such provision could be interpreted as the acme of the indigenisation policies, carried out in Nigeria ever since the acquisition of independence, with the principal aim of nationalising the main industrial sectors, fully controlled and managed by the European until then.

After a more careful analysis, however, Section 54(1) can be considered as one of the tools that MNCs can rely upon to avoid liability for harmful actions perpetrated within the Nigerian borders. Indeed, the fact that MNCs operate in Nigeria through subsidiaries which are legally incorporated under domestic law, gives way to problems related to the choice of jurisdiction in the event of disputes arising from the breach of the contracts or – as was the case in *Akpan v Royal Dutch Shell Plc*[16] – from the attempt to obtain compensation for damages caused to the communities' livelihoods.

In his commentary to this case, McConnell gives an exhaustive overview of the international doctrine regarding the attribution of such liability. To be more precise, the author underlines that, although the UN Secretary General's 2009 Special Representative for Business and Human Rights' Framework confers to the states the

---

[16] *Akpan v Royal Dutch Shell Plc* [2013] No. 337050/HA ZA 09-1580 (District Court of the Hague).

primary "responsibility to protect their citizens from corporate actors' "[17] possibly dangerous activities, often states "lack the resources to do so, or may even be complicit in violations."[18]

Despite adhering to the "international trend holding parent companies liable for the harmful practices of their foreign subsidiaries",[19] the Dutch court – in front of which the case was brought by four Nigerian plaintiffs in a joint action with Friends of the Earth Netherlands – manifested doubts as whether, in the case the allegations against the parent company (Royal Dutch Shell) were dismissed, the claims against the Nigerian subsidiary (Shell Petroleum Development Company Nigeria – SPDC) were to be dismissed, too, on the grounds of lack of jurisdiction.

Even though the Dutch court decided that such dismissal was not appropriate, this cannot be regarded as a well-established juridical trend.

Furthermore, it has been observed that the fact that the Nigerian government is a partner of the MNCs in their oil development projects (another measure – beside the domestic incorporation of subsidiaries contained in the CAMA – which is supposed to work for the indigenisation of the oil industry in the country[20]), is deleterious for the genuine work of the regulatory agencies, and, as a result, for the

---

[17] Sanctioned, amongst others, by the United Nations Draft Norms on the Responsibilities of Transnational Corporations and Other Business Enterprises with Regard to Human Rights.

[18] L J McConnell, 'Establishing liability for multinational oil companies in parent/subsidiary relationships' [2014] ELR 50, 51.
Pertaining to this – and highlighting the peculiarly intricate situation in the management of the oil sector in Nigeria – Ploch stresses the point of the political complicity in the criminal activities related to oil: the deriving proceeds are used for the funding of electoral campaigns and other political activities. See: Ploch, 'Nigeria: Current Issues and U.S. Policy' (Federation of American Scientists 2012). Available at: <http://fas.org/sgp/crs/row/RL33964.pdf> accessed on 15 July 2014.

[19] Ibid.

[20] In this regard, it is possible to link the discussion to the opinion of Ogutuga, who argues that the transposition of international law instruments into national law has to be carried out in a particularly careful way in the developing countries. See: M Ogutuga, 'CSR obligations of Transnational Corporations and legal enforcement mechanisms in extractive industries: how effective are these mechanisms in the protection of Human Rights in Africa?' [2009] CELMPM Annual Review, Vol.13.

genuine enforcement of regulations in the field.[21] This is the reason why the Revenue Watch Institute has observed that, if the proposed Petroleum Industry Bill will fail to amend the disclosure provisions for the state-owned companies, its efforts for a higher transparency in the Nigerian oil sector will be vain.[22]

The next paragraph will analyse the amendments put forward by this Bill and its main shortcomings.

Beside the issue of foreign businesses' incorporation into Nigerian law, the CAMA also deals with the question of disclosure. Amao (backed up by Ejims and Villiers) observes that the disclosure requirements only encompass duties to the companies' shareholders, evidencing an approach that, more in general, emerges from the typical structure and wording of the investment contracts between MNCs and Nigeria.[23]

Amao stresses that, according to Section 279, "company directors owe duties only to the company (interpreted as its shareholders), and therefore have no legal responsibility or capacity to embark on any other duty apart from their duty to the company and its shareholders." Moreover, "the directors' report requirement under

---

[21] As an example, see: E Oshionebo, 'Transnational corporations, civil society organisations and social accountability in Nigeria's oil and gas industry' [2007] AJICL 107, 108.
[22] Sayne, Mahdavi, Heller, Schreuder, 'The Petroleum Industry Bill and the Future of NNPC' (RevenueWatch.org 2012) available at:<http://www.revenuewatch.org/publications/petroleum-industry-bill-and-future-nnpc> accessed on 14 February 2014.
[23] See: O O Amao , 'Corporate Social Responsibility, Multinational Corporations and the Law in Nigeria: Controlling Multinationals in Host States' [2008] JAL 52 89-113,
O Ejims, 'The impact of Nigerian international petroleum contracts on environmental and human rights of indigenous communities' [2013] AJICL 345, 349, and
C Villiers, *Corporate Reporting and Company Law* (1st, Cambridge University Press, e.g. Oxford 2006), xi.

Section 342 of the CAMA relates solely to the company's financial performance [...]."[24]

It is possible to argue that the two above-mentioned provisions reflect a general paradigm in the current trend regarding the drafting of commercial agreements between multinational companies and developing countries. This trend can be described as based on an "overly commercial approach",[25] which does not take into account the interests of the communities living in the areas where the development projects take place.

This paragraph has analysed how the CAMA affects, firstly, the attribution of liability to subsidiaries and parent companies in the event of problems arising from oil operations, and, secondly, the possibility to access corporations' documents.

The two matters are of crucial importance to understand how multinational oil enterprises behave when faced with claims by local people. In addition, the way in which the CAMA is drafted further prevents individuals and groups from participating in the oil development.

### 1.1.4. The Petroleum Industry Bill (PIB) 2007-2012

First proposed in 2007, the PIB is still under the Nigerian National Assembly's examination. In essence, the PIB seeks to reform the structure and the functions of the Nigeria National Petroleum Corporation (NNPC). One of its main intended outcomes is to enhance the transparency and the accountability of the state-owned

---

[24] Both quotes are from: O O Amao, supra note 23, p. 101.
[25] O Ejims, supra note 23, p. 349.
As regards the particular issue of the disclosure of corporate documents, see: C Villiers, supra note 23, xi.

oil company, by devolving some of its functions to independent agencies, and, by doing so, to possibly improve the transparency of the whole petroleum sector in the country.

This would be a natural consequence of the PIB, given the fact that the main avenue for the realisation of oil projects in Nigeria is the formation of joint-ventures between NNPC (i.e. the government[26]) and the foreign MNCs.

Thus, reforming the structure and the responsibilities of NNPC would also push the government to assume its own responsibilities: so far, it has taken advantage of the uncertainty surrounding the oil industry in the country, to the detriment of local communities.

However, as the Revenue Watch Institute has argued, there are various loopholes in the PIB provisions: firstly, the National Petroleum Assets Management Corporation (NPAMC) and the National Gas Company Plc. (NGC) "are not subject to the upstream contract-disclosure requirement, which means that joint ventures and gas contracts will *likely remain opaque*"[27] (emphasis added); secondly, "the downstream regulator is not required to publish information on downstream activities"[28]; thirdly, "there are no auditing requirements for NNPC and NGC, and NPAMC is required to publish only a summary of its audited accounts."[29]

---

[26] As noted by Oshionebo: "Because [...] the government is in joint-ventures partnership with oil and gas [MNCs] enforcement of regulation is sometimes viewed by the government as detrimental to its investment in its joint-venture projects. Thus, in order to safeguard their position, regulatory officials have to be careful not to step on government toes." See: E Oshionebo, supra note 21, p. 108.
[27] Sayne, Mahdavi, Heller, Schreuder, supra note 22.
[28] Ibid.

[29] Ibid.

In conclusion, the drafting of the PIB does not seem to bring the much needed comprehensive reconsideration of the current applicable disclosure requirements provisions into the Nigerian law.

## 1. 2. Niger Delta Development Commission (NDDC) Act 2000

The NDDC was created in 2000 with the basic aim of establishing a new regulatory body for an enhanced effectiveness in the management of oil development in the region. In particular, the title of the Act highlights the importance of addressing the "ecological problems which arise from the exploration of oil minerals in the Niger-Delta area [...]."[30]

Section 2(1)(b) of the NDDC Act sets the rules for the composition of the Commission. Such rules reflect the need for a stronger representation of the oil producing states; Section 2(1)(d) calls for a deeper integration and cooperation between these states and oil operators. In addition, Section 2(1)(c) provides for the representation of non-oil producing states.[31]

The main criticisms of the NDDC Act will be analysed in paragraphs 2.1. and 2.2. below.

---

[30] Niger Delta Development Commission (Establishment etc.) Act 2000. Available at: <http://www.commonlii.org/ng/legis/num_act/ndcea504/> accessed on 13 July 2014.
[31] One of the most challenging problems of modern Nigeria, is the division between the northern and the southern part of the country. The concentration of the oil production in the Niger Delta is one of the reasons for the political and social unrest in the North. See for instance: Ahmed, 'Behind the rise of Boko Haram - ecological disaster, oil crisis, spy games Islamist militancy in Nigeria is being strengthened by western and regional fossil fuel interests' (theguardian.com last update 2014). Available at: <http://www.theguardian.com/environment/earth-insight/2014/may/09/behind-rise-nigeria-boko-haram-climate-disaster-peak-oil-depletion> accessed on 11 August 2014.

## 1. 3. <u>International instruments</u>

This paragraph will study the international instruments adopted by Nigeria in the field of human rights protection and MNCs' activities regulation and their effects in the country, taking into consideration whether they have been transposed into national law or not, and the ways in which such transposition has been implemented.[32]

Section 12(1) of the Nigerian Constitution, states that the transposition into national law of an international law instrument is the *sine qua non* for the implementation of such instruments in the country.[33]

As summed up by the University of Minnesota, although Nigeria has signed many of the international law instruments in the field of human rights, its various governments have not ratified nor implemented them.[34]

It is important to stress the fact that the preamble of the United Nations Draft Norms on the Responsibilities of Transnational Corporations and Other Business

---

[32] Among the main international human rights treaties signed by Nigeria, the following are the most important: ICCPR (International Covenant on Civil and Political Rights), the ICESCR (International Covenant on Economic, Social, and Cultural Rights) – both adopted by the UN General Assembly in 1966, the International Convention on the Elimination of All forms of Racial Discrimination (ICERD) – adopted by the UN General Assembly in 1965, and the Convention Against Torture and Other Cruel, Inhuman or Degrading Treatment or Punishment (CAT), adopted by the UN General Assembly in 1984.

[33] This constitutional provision can be interpreted in the view of the need, on the part of developing countries, to revise international law provision before they transfer part of their sovereignty. Pertaining to this, Ogutuga points out that, in spite of the provisions contained in the United Nations Draft Norms on the Responsibilities of Transnational Corporations and Other Business Enterprises with Regard to Human Rights, lesser developed countries must be cautious in setting their legal structure that apply to TNCs. In other words, "TNCs investing in the poorer developing countries usually take advantage of weak laws and standards [there], and thereby lower their standards of practice, thereby deviating from international standards, or standards of practice of their own countries." See: M Ogutuga, supra note 20, p. 23.

[34] See University of Minnesota. Human Rights Library, 'Ratification of International Human Rights Treaties - Nigeria' (umn.edu 2012 – last update). Available at: <http://www1.umn.edu/humanrts/research/ratification-nigeria.html> accessed on 15 July 2014.

Enterprises with Regard to Human Rights (hereinafter UN Norms[35]) recalls a series of international conventions on human rights. Therefore, it is necessary to strongly highlight that the mentioned Nigerian deficiency regarding the transposition of such international legal instruments into national law, deprives the signing of both those treaties and the UN Norms (which seek to apply the provisions contained in the former to the social behaviour of international businesses) of their effectiveness.

Section A.1. (General Obligations) of the mentioned UN Norms sanctions that:

> "*States have the primary responsibility* to promote, secure the fulfilment of, respect, ensure respect of, and protect human rights recognised in international as well as national law, *including assuring that transnational corporations and other business enterprises respect human rights*. Within their respective spheres of activity and influence, *transnational corporations and other business enterprises have the obligation* to promote, secure the fulfilment of, respect, ensure respect of, and protect human rights recognized in international as well as national law."[36] (Emphasis added).

This provision reflects the fact that the international legal personality is first of all attributed to national states. Notwithstanding the fact that, nowadays, other institutions, such as international organisations, are regarded to have international legal personality, "the doctrine has not expanded to include wholly-private companies."[37]

As will be further described in this study, and as McConnell has observed: "[...] while a state may well possess a duty to protect its citizens, it may lack the resources to do so, or may be *complicit* in such violations."[38] (Emphasis added). In other words, and in particular regard to the Nigerian case, although the state is the responsible

---

[35] Adopted in 2003 by the UN Sub-commission on the Promotion and Protection of Human Rights.
[36] See: UN Draft Norms on the Responsibilities of Transnational Corporations and Other Business Enterprises with Regard to Human Rights, E/CN.4/Sub.2/2003/12 (2003) Available at:
<http://www1.umn.edu/humanrts/links/NormsApril2003.html> Accessed on 12 July 2014.
[37] See: L J McConnell, supra note 18, p. 89.
[38] Ibid. See supra p. 22.

institution for the protection of human rights within its national borders, it may not have the capability and/or the willingness to do so.[39]

Section E.10 (Respect for National Sovereignty and Human Rights) of the UN Norms states that:

> "Transnational corporations [...] shall recognize and respect applicable norms of international law; national laws; regulations; administrative practices; the rule of law; the public interest; development objectives; social, economic, and cultural policies including transparency, accountability, and prohibition of corruption; and authority of the countries in which the enterprises operate."

With particular regard to environmental protection, Section G.14 puts an obligation upon transnational corporations to comply with international and national provisions in order to preserve the environment of the countries in which they operate.

Remarkably, Section G.14 considers environmental preservation and human rights protection at the same level. This is of crucial importance in the analysis of the corporate behaviour in Nigeria, where the violations of human rights often occur through the breach of environmental obligations.

## I. 4. Concluding remarks

The analysis carried out so far will serve as a background to the next chapters, since it will represent the basis on which further study on the peculiarities of the country will be conducted, with particular regard to the correlation between oil

---

[39] In 2012, the Congressional Research Service released a report on Nigeria, which reveals that "according to recent estimates, about 10% of Nigerian oil is taken away from the market every year. [...] It is proven that local politicians have funded their activities and electoral campaigns with money made by means of these criminal activities." See: Ploch, 'Nigeria: Current Issues and U.S. Policy' (Federation of American Scientists 2012), 13. Available at: <http://fas.org/sgp/crs/row/RL33964.pdf> accessed on 15 July 2014.

MNCs' practices and the environmental disaster in the Niger Delta and the Nigerian human rights performance.

## 2. Oil, environment and human rights

Numerous observers have highlighted the correlation between the socio-political and ethnical structure of Nigeria and the landscape of conflict and instability which characterises the oil sector in the country.[40] Such conflict for the ownership and control of natural resources is both the cause and the effect of the displacement of people, arising from the appropriation of land for oil development.

This chapter will analyse the negative consequences of the oil multinationals' activities in Nigeria from a perspective which will go beyond the mere observation of the legal *status quo*, looking at the ways in which these activities have negatively influenced the Nigerian landscape through the glasses of history, politics, and ethnical inequalities.

### 2. 1. Ethnicity, oil, displacement

Out of 170 million Nigerian citizens, more than 62% live in "extreme poverty".[41]

The root of this situation can be found in the political, administrative and ethnical asset of the country. Nigeria is a federation, where the boundaries between the various states are mainly drawn on the basis of ethnical differences.

---

[40] E.g.: C Obi and S A Rustad, *Oil and Insurgency in the Niger Delta, Managing the complex politics of petro-violence* (1st, Zed Books Ltd., Uppsala, Sweden 2011), and
P Maass, *Crude World, The violent twilight of oil* (1st, Alfred A. Knopf, New York 2009).
[41] CIA, supra note 2.

The ethnical division led to a weak sentiment of national unity; such weakness is the most fundamental ground for the current situation.

In describing the conflicting scenario of the Niger Delta region, Obi and Rustad have noted that:

> "[After Nigeria was transformed into a federation] the institutionalization of revenue sharing, political representation and power distribution along [...] regional lines reinforced ethnic majority hegemony, and rivalry, which also meant that ethnic minorities often lost out, or were marginalized, in the power equation at the regional and national level.
> [...] after the Nigerian civil war, [...] the Niger Delta['s oil] [...] became the main source of national revenues and export earnings."[42]

Moreover, in 1969 (three years after the attempted secession in Biafra[43]), the military government passed the already mentioned Petroleum Act, which vested "the entire ownership and control of all petroleum [...] in the State."[44]

Hence, the oil development projects in the Niger Delta started without any participation of, or consultation to, the local communities, since they had no say in the matter.

---

[42] C Obi and S A Rustad, supra note 40, pp. 5-6.
Peter Maass elucidates the current Nigerian situation. According to him, every conflicting party share the same interest in avoiding a stop of the oil activities in the country, since they all take economic advantage from the oil flow – not only oil companies, but also the rebels, who damage the pipelines after having bribed the military in order to avoid their intervention.
Even the military, have their own role: they are paid not to intervene when the bunkered oil has to be smuggled outside the country.
Maass concludes that federal and local governments, armed forces and rebel militias are both fighting against each other and making business together. See: P Maass, supra note 40, pp. 73-74.
Philippe Le Billon stresses the following point: "[in the Nigerian case, it is possible to identify] a breakdown of rebel and government categories, and multiple financial flows linking oil and perpetrators of violence-for example with blurred categories between armed militants and (former) thugs working for well-established politicians." See: P Le Billon, 'Oil and Armed Conflict in Africa' [2012] Afr. Geo. Rev. 29 1 63, 81.
[43] Pertaining to this, a comprehensive analysis can be found in S K Panter-Brick, 'The Right to Self-determination: its application to Nigeria' [1968] International Affairs (Royal Institute of International Affairs 1944) 44:2 254-266.
[44] Petroleum Act of the Federal Republic of Nigeria 1969, S 1(1).

Nwapi finds that the origin of the internal instability surrounding the oil sector lies, again, in the legal provisions: the root of local discontent is to be found in the lack of local people engagement (in any of the phases of the oil development decision-making and actual realisation of oil facilities and infrastructures) in the mentioned NDDC Act (which was supposed to remedy to this vacuum in the law).[45] Although it was intended to be a remedy to this state of affairs, its main critical point is that it "makes no provision for the participation of local communities in the planning and execution of the commission's projects."[46]

The environmental damage caused to the region by oil activities is the main reason of internal displacement. Opukri and Ibaba describe the situation as follows: "It is discernible that farmers and fishermen, whose farmlands and fisheries are affected, have no alternative than to move to other areas as displaced people, at least for a period. [...] [People] are forced to migrate [...] because there is no alternative."[47] The intensity of migration to the big urban centres is boosted by the critical environmental situation.[48]

There is some uncertainty about the exact number of Internally Displaced People (IDP) in the country and some institutions do not even report this category

---

[45] C Nwapi, 'A legislative proposal for public participation in oil and gas decision-making in Nigeria' [2010] JAL 184, 187, and
N E Ojukwu-Ogba, 'Legislating development in Nigeria's oil producing region: the NDDC Act sever years on' [2009] AJICL 136, 137.
[46] C Nwapi, supra note 45, p. 187.
[47] See: C O Opukri and I S Ibaba, 'Oil induced environmental degradation and internal population displacement in the Niger Delta' [e.g. 2005] JSDA 185, 188.
[48] B A Ahonsi, 'Capacity and governance deficits in the response to the Niger Delta crisis' in C Obi and S A Rustad (eds), Oil and insurgency in the Niger Delta, Managing the complex politics of petro-violence (1st, Zed Books Ltd., Uppsala, Sweden 2011), 30.

in their statistics. Although the UNHCR[49] recognises the overwhelming problem of forced migration in Nigeria, it is curious that it does not observe any internally displaced person[50] residing in the country. Instead, the federal government of Nigeria (through its National Emergency Management Agency – NEMA), acknowledges the presence of 16,470 internally displaced people living in the dedicated camps.[51] It has to be noted that, however, the governmental Agency does not mention oil exploitation as one of the causes behind the internal displacement.

In addition, according to the Internal Displaced People Monitoring Centre and the Norwegian Refugee Council, Nigeria is included in the list of those countries which have up to 50,000 people displaced, but this data only takes into account displacement caused by natural disasters.[52]

Nonetheless, Human Rights Watch clearly points out the link between oil activities in the Niger Delta with the inter-communal ant inter-ethnic violence in the region, which, in turn, causes the displacement of people.[53]

Beside the aspect of environmental disaster, another important cause of instability, endemic violence and displacement in the Niger Delta region is the uneven allocation of oil revenues: the wealth generated through oil royalties, paid by

---

[49] United Nations High Commissioner for Refugees.
[50] According to UNHCR, "unlike refugees, Internally Displaced Persons (IDPs) have not crossed an international border to find sanctuary but have remained inside their home countries. Even if they have fled for similar reasons as refugees (armed conflict, generalized violence, human rights violations), IDPs legally remain under the protection of their own government – even though that government might be the cause of their flight. As citizens, they retain all of their rights and protection under both human rights and international humanitarian law." UNHCR, 'Internally Displaced People, On the run in their own land' (unhcr.org 2014). Available at: <http://www.unhcr.org/pages/49c3646c146.html> accessed on 13 July 2014.
[51] National Emergency Management Agency, '16,470 Persons still in IDP camps' (nema.gov 2014). Available at: <http://nema.gov.ng/16470-displaced-persons-still-in-idp-camps/> accessed on 13 July 2014.
[52] UNHCR, 'Global Estimates 2011, People displaced by natural hazard-induced disasters' (unhcr.org 2011). Available at: <http://www.unhcr.org/50f95fcb9.html> accessed on 13 July 2014
[53] See for instance: Human Rights Watch, 'The Warri Crisis, Fueling Violence' (hrw.org 2003). Available at: <http://www.hrw.org/node/12203/section/2> accessed on 14 July 2014.

the operating companies and collected by the federal state, has neither been properly redistributed nor efficiently invested in the sustainable development of the country.[54]

## 2. 2. The unsustainability of oil development in Nigeria

*The State shall protect and improve the environment and safeguard the water, air, land, forest and wildlife of Nigeria.*[55]

Constitution of Nigeria.

As seen with regards to the NDDC Act, one of the objectives of the Commission is to achieve a sustainable development in the region.[56]

Nevertheless, despite the efforts made by the government in this direction, much work has to be done in order to ensure the fulfilment of this goal.[57] The marine biodiversity which used to distinguish the Niger Delta and to be the basis of both the alimentation and economy of local communities, has been destroyed by the pollution caused – on the one hand – by vandalism perpetrated towards the oil infrastructures, and – on the other hand – by the negligence of oil multinationals themselves.

Oil spills are not the only hazards caused by the oil and gas industry in Nigeria: construction of roads, felling of forests, gas flaring, waste, and increased migration

---

[54] On this issue, see: I S Ibaba, 'The Ijaw National Congress and conflict resolution in the Niger Delta' in C Obi and S A Rustad (eds), *Oil and insurgency in the Niger Delta, Managing the complex politics of petro-violence* (1st, Zed Books Ltd., Uppsala, Sweden 2011).
[55] Article 20, Constitution of the Federal Republic of Nigeria.
[56] For instance, Section 7(1)(b) states: [The Commission shall] conceive, plan and implement, in accordance with set rules and regulations, projects and programmes for the of the Niger-Delta area in the field of transportation including roads, jetties and waterways, health, education, employment, industrialization, agriculture and fisheries, housing and urban development, water supply, electricity and telecommunications.
[57] N E Ojukwu-Ogba, supra note 45.

are also of major impact on the environment of the Niger Delta. Rural communities have been subject to the most harmful consequences.[58] The National Policy on Environment, adopted in 1989, states indeed:

> "[The] sustainable development of the oil and gas sector is [...] of utmost importance, especially since virtually all of the activities in both the upstream and downstream sectors are *not only pollution-prone, but readily provoke social discord.*"[59] (Emphasis added).

As already noted, the current situation is worsened by the fact that local communities, especially when organised in rebel movements and militias, resort to action of disturbance, namely oil bunkering.

However, it is undisputable that the adoption of *double standards* by the oil companies operating in Nigeria[60] is the most important factor in determining the present situation in the Niger Delta.

The stance of the oil multinationals on this subject is summarised by the World Bank, which argued in 1995:

> "Oil pollution, contrary to common perception, is only of moderate priority when compared with the full spectrum of environmental problems in the Niger Delta. [...]."[61]

---

[58] See for instance: Apata, 'Linkages between Crude-oil Exploration and Agricultural Development in Nigeria: Implications for relevant qualitative data collection and analysis to improve rural economy.' (fao.org 2010) Available at:
<http://www.fao.org/fileadmin/templates/ess/pages/rural/wye_city_group/2010/May/WYE_2010.4.3_Apata.pdf> accessed 12 August 2014.

[59] Federal Environment Protection Agency, 'National Policy on the Environment' (nesrea.org 1998). Available at: <http://www.nesrea.org/images/National%20Policy%20on%20Environment.pdf> accessed on 14 July 2014, S 4.14.

[60] As to say, the recurrent practice of setting a lower standard of conduct as concerns their environmental performance in Nigeria compared to the usual standard in the developed countries.

[61] Universitat Pompeu Fabra Barcelona, 'Nigeria: Issues and dilemmas' (econ.epf.edu 2004). Available at: <http://www.econ.upf.edu/~lemenestrel/IMG/pdf/shell_nigeria_website-2.pdf> Accessed on 2 August 2014.
What clearly emerges here is a lack of objectivity on the part of the World Bank, since it is quite hard to understand how dams and population increases can compete against oil activities as the main source of pollution in the Niger Delta.

In this regard, in 2009 Amnesty International pointed out that "[people] living in the Niger Delta have to drink, cook with, and wash in polluted water; they eat fish contaminated with oil and other toxins [...]."[62]

The United Nations Environment Programme (UNEP) *Environmental Assessment of Ogoniland*, clarifies that:

> "[The] control, maintenance and decommissioning of oilfield infrastructure in Ogoniland are inadequate. Industry best practices and SPDC own procedures have not been applied, creating public safety issues. [...] while the [last] changes are an improvement, they still do not meet the local regulatory requirements or international best practices."[63]

The main goal of the National Oil Spill Detection and Response Agency (NOSDRA)[64] is to implement the National Oil Spill Contingency Plan (NOSCP) for Nigeria in the view of the fulfilment of the requirements set by the International Convention on Oil Pollution Preparedness, Response and Co-operation 1990.[65] However, as recognised by Ekhator, the policy which constitutes the basis of NOSDRA "has no force of law, and sanctions cannot be meted to firms who are in breach of the policy."[66]

Section 27(1) of the National Environmental Standards and Regulations Enforcement Agency (NESREA) Establishment Act 2007 has been criticised by

---

[62] Amnesty International, 'Nigeria: Petroleum, Pollution and Poverty in the Niger Delta' (amnesty.org 2009). Available at: <http://www.amnesty.org/en/library/asset/AFR44/017/2009/en/e2415061-da5c-44f8-a73c-a7a4766ee21d/afr440172009en.pdf> accessed on14 July 2014. P. 21.

[63] United Nations Environment Programme, 'Environmental Assessment of Ogoniland' (unep.org 2011). Available at: <http://postconflict.unep.ch/publications/OEA/UNEP_OEA.pdf> accessed on18 June 2014. P. 12

[64] Created in 2006, by means of the Act which is called after the Agency itself.

[65] Adopted by the International Maritime Organisation in 1990 and entered into force in 1995.

[66] E Osa Ekhator, 'Environmental Protection in the oil and gas industry in Nigeria: the roles of governmental agencies' [2013] IELR 196, 203.

Oshionebo inasmuch as it "prohibits the discharge of hazardous substances only if they are on 'harmful quantities'".[67] According to the author, "it is doubtful whether the NESREA has the capacity to determine [...] the quantities of hazardous substances that qualify as 'harmful' given its institutional deficiencies, including its lack of expertise and equipment."[68]

MNCs, moreover, do not seem frankly committed to the clean-up of the region, as emerges from the cited UNEP *Environmental Assessment of Ogoniland*. Amnesty International reports that local NGOs have been blaming oil operators for "designating [otherwise] controllable spills as sabotage in order to avoid liability for compensation."[69]

Without a comprehensive revision of the legal framework on environmental rights, the achievement of a sustainable development in the Niger Delta will remain an unrealistic goal.

---

[67] E Oshionebo, *Regulating transnational corporations in domestic and international regimes an African case study*, University of Toronto Press Inc., Toronto 2009. 57.
[68] Ibid.
[69] Amnesty International, supra note 62, p. 15.

## 2. 3. The human rights performance

*Businesses should support and respect the protection of internationally proclaimed human rights; and make sure that they are not complicit in human rights abuses.*

The 1st and 2nd principles of the United Nations Global Compact.[70]

*2.3.1. International standards and domestic non-compliance*

As seen earlier in this study, the usual drafting of the contracts for the exploitation of petroleum resources between oil MNCs and the government of Nigeria does not take into account the rights of those who live nearby the areas identified as suitable for oil development projects.

This situation arises from the described Nigerian legal framework which vests in the government all the rights on land, basically leaving the local communities bereft of any right.

Such legal architecture blatantly infringes upon the internationally accepted doctrine on the indigenous peoples' rights.

The analysis of Articles 26 and 32 of the United Nations Declaration on the Rights of Indigenous People (UNDRIP)[71] reveals that the indigenous peoples' rights to own land and resources, as well as to develop these land and resources, and to be protected and consulted by states when they aim to use land and resources for the development of the national economy, are well-established in the international law doctrine.[72] However, Nigeria abstained from voting for this Convention.[73]

---

[70] See: UN Global Compact, 'Global Corporate Sustainability Report' (unglobalcompact.org 2013). Available at:
<http://www.unglobalcompact.org/docs/about_the_gc/Global_Corporate_Sustainability_Report2013.pdf> accessed 16 June 2014.
[71] Issued with Resolution of the General Assembly No. 61/295.
[72] Article 26 of the UN Declaration on Indigenous People, indeed, sanctions that: 1. Indigenous

A provision concerning the right of all peoples to "freely dispose of their natural wealth and resources"[74] is also contained in Article 1 of the International Covenant on Civil and Political Rights (ICCPR). Such right is integral part of the right to self-determination, proclaimed in point 1 of the same article. But, although the country accessed this international agreement in 1993, Nigeria has not yet ratified it either.[75]

The following is an interpretation of the provisions contained in Articles 21, 24, and 16 of the African Charter on Human and Peoples' Rights (ACHPR).[76] For the purposes of this study, this interpretation is significant inasmuch as it shows the importance of the Charter, in the view of the empowerment of local communities and peoples, with the aim of involving them in the development of their own territories and resources.

According to Article 21, indeed, all the peoples have the right to "freely dispose of their wealth and natural resources" – a right of which peoples "shall never be

---

peoples have the right to the lands, territories and resources which they have traditionally owned, occupied or otherwise used or acquired. 2. Indigenous peoples have the right to own, use, develop and control the lands, territories and resources that they possess by reason of traditional ownership or other traditional occupation or use, as well as those which they have otherwise acquired. 3. States shall give legal recognition and protection to these lands, territories and resources. Such recognition shall be conducted with due respect to the customs, traditions and land tenure systems of the indigenous peoples concerned.
Article 32 compels the States to "consult and cooperate [...] with the indigenous peoples concerned in order to obtain their free and informed consent prior to the approval of any project affecting their lands or territories and other resources, particularly in connection with the development, utilization or exploitation of mineral, water or other resources."
[73] The Nigerian representative (Mr. Akindele) – despite his welcoming to the broadness of the Declaration – declared that "A number of concerns that were critical to his country's interests [...] had not been satisfactorily addressed, including the issue of self-determination and the control of lands, territories and resources." He also added that "Nigeria would continue to promote the issue of indigenous people's rights, culture and dignity."
See: UN General Assembly, 'General Assembly adopts Declaration on Rights of Indigenous Peoples' (un.org 2007). Available at: <http://www.un.org/News/Press/docs/2007/ga10612.doc.htm> accessed on 15 July 2014.
[74] ICCPR. Article 1(2).
[75] University of Minnesota, supra note 34.
[76] Adopted by the African Union in 1981 and entered into force in 1986.

deprived of" without being given the possibility to recover their property, or compensated for their losses; Article 24 states that "all peoples shall have the right to a general satisfactory environment favourable to their development". Article 16, finally, puts the states under the obligation to ensure the health of the peoples.

In the decision of the African Commission on Human and Peoples' Rights on the case *Social and Economic Rights Action Centre (SERAC) and Another v Nigeria*[77], the Commission found that the Nigerian government was infringing Article 24 (and, it is contended here, Articles 21 and 16) of the Charter, by allowing oil MNCs to carry out operations causing major environmental degradation and consequently affecting the health of the people of Ogoniland and their right to decide about the exploitation of their own resources.[78]

As pointed out by Atsegbua, "Article 24 of the [ACHPR], which recognises environmental right as a human right can be relied upon by a Nigerian to enforce his environmental right instead of relying on section 20 of the 1999 Constitution which is not justiciable."[79] By doing so, claimants can bypass the obstacle of the missing transposition and enforcement of other dedicated international instruments into Nigerian domestic law.[80]

Hence, relying on the ACHPR as an already enforceable legal instrument, can be regarded as an additional avenue for who seeks access to environmental justice in Nigeria. This opinion is shared by Egede, who notes that, in the African case law,

---

[77] *Social and Economic Rights Action Centre (SERAC) and Another v Nigeria* [2001] AHRLR 60 (ACHPR 2001).

[78] E Egede, 'Bringing human rights home: an examination of the domestication of human rights treaties in Nigeria' [2007] JAL 249, 265.

[79] L Atsegbua, supra note 5, pp. 89-92.

Section 20 is, in fact, included in chapter 2 of the Nigerian Constitution, which sets the Fundamental Objectives and directive Principles of State Policy.

[80] Ibid.

the Nigerian government has been considered in breach of the human right to a healthy environment, since it allows oil MNCs to cause environmental degradation.[81]

### 2.3.2. Oil multinational corporations' complicity in human rights violations

It is now appropriate to link the discussion about the Nigerian human rights performance with the multinationals' complicity issue, and to move on towards the analysis of the correlation between this feature and the lack of sustainable oil development in the country.

Richardson analyses the Complicity-based Doctrine, arguing that its essential scope is the analysis of the "direct involvement of actors in abusive conduct where another party commits the actual harm."[82] This scheme can be found in the *Wiwa v Royal Dutch Petroleum* case[83]: indeed, in his commentary to this case, Muchlinski has noted that the plaintiffs claimed that the defendant MNC was allegedly "supporting the Nigerian state in its repression of the Ogoni people through inter alia the supply of money, weapons and logistical support to the Nigerian military which carried out the abuses."[84]

Human Rights Watch puts it this way:

"[Oil] companies [...] share [...] responsibility for the human rights abuses taking place in the Niger Delta: *whether by action or omission they*

---

[81] E Egede, supra note 78, p. 284.
[82] B J Richardson, 'Socially Responsible Investing for Sustainability: Overcoming Its Incomplete and Conflicting Rationales', [2013] TEL 2:2 311-338, for a theoretical discussion about the definition and the interpretation of the Complicity Doctrine.
[83] *Wiwa v. Royal Dutch Petroleum Co.* [2001] 226 F.3d 88 (2d Cir. 2000), 532 U.S. 941.
[84] P T Muchlinski, 'Human rights and multinationals: is there a problem?' [2001] International Affairs 77:1 31, 41.

*play a role.* [...] All the oil companies operating in Nigeria share [the] responsibility to promote respect for human rights."[85] (Emphasis added).

It is a contention of this work that, since the voluntariness of CSR practices limits their influence,[86] the home states governments – as international legal persons responsible for the fulfilment of the international standards in the human rights field – should put more efforts on the abidance by these standards on the part of businesses based in their territories.

The importance of Nigerian oil for the global markets clearly emerges from the words of David Goldwin, former Coordinator of the International Energy Affairs in the US Department of State, who said that if Nigeria was able to exploit its full oil potential, this would represent an important contribution to lowering and stabilising the global oil price.[87]

The viewpoint according to which there is a strong link between oil MNCs and their home governments is shared by Soremekun, who quotes Obi: "[They are] guarantors of steady supply of cheap energy, employment for their citizens, profits for shareholders and revenue for their home governments."[88]

---

[85] Human Rights Watch, 'The Price of Oil. Corporate Social Responsibility and Human Rights Violations in Nigeria's Oil Producing Communities.' (hrw.org 1999). Available at:
<http://www.hrw.org/reports/1999/nigeria/nigeria0199.pdf> accessed on 16 July 2014, p.3.
Human Rights Watch reports the opinion of Shell about the issue. The International NGO states indeed: "Shell acknowledged that it had conducted these negotiations but stated that none of the purchases had been concluded. However, the company stated [...] that it 'cannot give an undertaking not to provide weapons in the future, as, due to the deteriorating security situation in Nigeria, we may want to see the weapons currently used by the Police who protect Shell people and property upgraded." (Ibid., p. 14).
[86] B J Richardson, supra note 82, p. 311.
[87] Raidt and Smith, 'Advancing U.S., African, and Global Interests: Security and Stability in the West African Maritime Domain' (atlanticcouncil.org 2010). Available at:
<http://www.atlanticcouncil.org/images/files/publication_pdfs/3/advancing-us-african-global-interests-security-stability-west-africa-maritime-domain.pdf> accessed on 19 July 2014.
[88] See: K Soremekun, 'Nigeria's oil diplomacy and the management of the Niger Delta's crisis' in C Obi and S A Rustad (eds), *Oil and insurgency in the Niger Delta, Managing the complex politics of petro-violence* (1st, Zed Books Ltd., Uppsala, Sweden 2011), 104.

From a legal point of view, however, it is not clear, nor is it well-established in the doctrine, "whether international law requires home states to help prevent human rights abuses abroad by corporations based within their territory."[89] Nonetheless, "[there] is greater consensus that those States are not prohibited from doing so where a recognized basis of jurisdiction exists."[90]

A suitable avenue to promote the fulfilment of human rights requirements both by nation states and MNCs would consist in a more vigorous impetus put on the implementation of the provisions contained in the Universal Declaration of Human Rights (UDHR) and in the UN Norms,[91] as well as of those included in the ACHPR.

The gradual process of considering the opportunity to assume the responsibility of MNCs' actions abroad, by their home states, has begun: the increasing disparities between developed and developing world fuel this process,[92] as well as the recognition of the fact that "business cannot flourish in an environment where fundamental human rights are not respected."[93]

---

[89] Sende, 'The Responsibilities of States for Actions of Transnational Corporations Affecting Social and Economic Rights: A Comparative Analysis of the Duty to Protect' (cjel.net 2009). Available at: <http://www.cjel.net/online/15_2-marsella-sende/> accessed on 1 August 2014.

[90] Ibid.

[91] The former, as it is possible to notice in the preamble, is not only addressed to nation states, but also to every *other organ of the society* (a broad category in which multinational enterprises – as well as other businesses – are obviously included).
Paragraph 1 of the latter provides as follows: "States have the primary responsibility to promote, secure the fulfilment of, respect, ensure respect of, and protect human rights recognised in international as well as national law, including assuring that *transnational corporations and other business enterprises respect human rights.* Within their respective spheres of activity and influence, *transnational corporations* and other business enterprises have the *obligation* to promote, secure the fulfilment of, respect, ensure respect of, and protect human rights recognized in international as well as national law." (Emphasis added).

[92] Muchlinski, P T *Multinational Enterprises and the Law* (2nd Edition). OUP, Oxford 2007, 516.

[93] Ibid.

Such considerations, by recognising the potential for good business embedded in the respect of human rights, also acknowledge the need for a more sustainable approach to development.

## 2. 4. <u>Concluding remarks</u>

As the above discussion attests, the need for a reallocation of priorities from the mere economic and political interests in the Nigerian oil, to a more responsible management of the industry – which would take into strong consideration the rights and interests of local peoples – emerges vehemently.

The analysis of the peculiar characteristics of Nigeria as a fragmented country, divided along ethnical, and socio-political lines, has been linked to the main legal issues concerning human and peoples' rights and the environment in the country, with the aim of showing the close liaison between these matters and the lack of commitment to a sustainable development by oil MNCs operating in Nigeria. The next chapter will explore how Corporate Social Responsibility can be enhanced in order to achieve such sustainable development in the Nigerian case.

# 3. CSR as a tool for sustainable development

This chapter will seek to explore how stronger, more accurate, and more binding social responsibility requirements would contribute to the development of the communities affected by decades of pollution and repression, and, through this, to the enhancement of the business environment in the country.

In pursuing this goal, the chapter will be structured in two subsections: firstly, attention will be paid to the relationship between self-regulation and legal regulation in the CSR scheme. Secondly, the discourse about participation and empowerment of local communities will be analysed.

## 3. 1. Self-regulation and legal regulation

It is a common perception that self-imposed corporations' codes of conduct are not sufficient. Although the mainstream corporate behaviour has been influenced by concepts of environmental and human rights protection, the prevalent business scheme, consisting in making the higher possible profit, still affects the corporate performance as concerns social responsibility.

It is possible to identify the fundamental deficiency of such codes of conduct in the fact that there is little scope for the enforcement of such standards. In the developing countries, additionally, public opinion is often unable to know about these voluntary corporate guidelines because of the want of access to information.[94]

---

[94] R Ntongho, 'Self-regulation of corporate governance in Africa: following the bandwagon?' ICCLR [2009] 20(2), 427-435.

In other words, the companies are not bound by their own codes of conduct, and, as such, they retain the discretion on the extent in which they are actually implemented.[95] As stressed by Oshionebo, "self-regulation will work best when it is undertaken against the background of vigorous state regulation."[96]

The Global Public Policy Institute offers a two-fold vision of the issue: if, on the one hand, regulation – both at the national and at the international level, is important, the horizontal cooperation amongst the involved actors (government, companies, civil society) is at least equally important.[97]

Peter Utting, of the UN Research Institute for Social Development, explains that the discourse about self-regulation and legal regulation finds a crucial node in the concept of Articulated Regulation. In other words, "the interface between soft and hard, and voluntary and legalistic, approaches"[98] is crucial in regulating CSR; moreover, such interface should be accompanied by "confrontation and collaboration, as well as [by a] greater policy coherence at both the micro level of the firm and the macro level of government and international policy".[99]

---

[95] M Ogutuga, supra note 20, p. 4.

[96] E Oshionebo, see supra note 21, p. 108.

[97] Benner and Witte, 'Rules for Global Players? Governing multinational corporations in developing countries'. (gppi.net 2006). Available at: < http://www.gppi.net/fileadmin/gppi/IP_Benner-Whitte.pdf> accessed on 1 August 2014.
See also: D Graham and N Woods, 'Making Corporate Self-Regulation Effective in Developing Countries' [2006] World Development 34:5, 868–883.

[98] Utting, 'Rethinking Business Regulation. From Self-Regulation to Social Control' (unrisd.org 2005), p. 1. Available at:
<http://www.unrisd.org/80256B3C005BCCF9/(httpAuxPages)/F02AC3DB0ED406E0C12570A10029B EC8/$file/utting.pdf> accessed on 14 August 2014.

[99] Ibid.

From the analysis of the codes of conduct of two of the main oil MNCs operating in Nigeria,[100] it is possible to note their excessive vagueness. To put this point differently, the structure and wording of such documents do not take into account the utmost importance of:

a) the differences between developed and developing countries;

b) the differences existing among developing countries themselves.

The cumulative effect of, on the one hand, such indefiniteness and, on the other hand, the lack of proper enforcement mechanisms in the developing countries, is the root of the different MNCs' implementation of the codes of conduct according to different legal, political, social and environmental backgrounds.[101]

The Nigerian National Assembly has been promoting a CSR Bill since 2008, which would seek to codify the provisions – mainly related to environmental protection – contained in various Acts,[102] and to establish a CSR Commission.[103]

---

[100] See: Shell, 'Code of Conduct' (shell.com 2010). Available at:
<http://www.shell.com/global/aboutshell/who-we-are/our-values/code-of-conduct.html > and
Chevron, 'Business Conduct and Ethics Code' (chevron.com 2014). Available at:
<http://www.chevron.com/documents/pdf/chevronbusinessconductethicscode.pdf>. Both accessed on 30 July 2014.

[101] Adomokai and Sheate clearly describe that environment and society are closely linked in the Nigerian local communities' perspective. See: R Adomokai, W R Sheate, 'Community participation and environmental decision-making in the Niger Delta' [2004] EIAR 24 495-518.
The same view point is shared by the United Nations. See: A I Osuoka, 'Oil and Gas Revenues and Development Challenges for the Niger Delta in Nigeria, Expert Group Meeting on the Use of Non-Renewable Energy Resource Revenues for Sustainable Local Development' (un.org 2007). Available at:
<http://www.un.org/esa/sustdev/sdissues/institutional_arrangements/egm2007/presentations/isaac
Osuoka.pdf> accessed on 14 July 2014, and
UN Interagency Framework Team for Preventive Action, 'Renewable Resources and Conflict. Toolkit and Guidance for Managing Land and Natural Resources Conflict' (un.org 2012). Available at:
<http://www.un.org/en/events/environmentconflictday/pdf/GN_Renewable_Consultation.pdf>
accessed on 1 August 2014.

[102] Such as, among others, the National Environmental Standards and Regulations Enforcement Agency (Establishment) Act 2007, or the Harmful Waste (Special Criminal Provision Act).

[103] See A Okoye, 'Exploring the relationship between corporate social responsibility, law and

Amongst the functions of the Commission, the creation of a standard for CSR, consistent with international standards,[104] is a remarkable provision in the view of a more stringent compliance to supranational rules by Nigeria; moreover, the Bill calls for the integration of CSR requirements into bilateral, regional and multilateral agreements.[105]

Sections 5(1)(c), 5(1)(e), and 5(1)(h) contain provisions related to the corporations' commitment to consult and work with host communities: according to Section 5(1)(c), indeed, the Commission shall conduct research and investigation of needs of host communities of corporate organisations; Section 5(1)(e), moreover, states that the Commission shall identify socially responsible behaviour in compliance with national and community legislation on equality and non-discrimination in all activities. Finally, Section 5(1)(h), provides that the Commission shall publish annual reports on social and environmental impacts of companies' direct activities on communities; and develop policies to encourage corporate organisations to undertake community engagements as part of corporate social responsibility, and ensure that companies sponsor cultural and educational activities that offer added value to Nigeria's socio-political and technological development. The Bill also prescribes that the cost of a company's total corporate social

---

development in an African context: should government be responsible for ensuring corporate responsibility?' [2012] IJLM, and

C Mordi, I S Opoyemi, M Tonbara, S Ojo, 'Corporate Social Responsibility and the Legal Regulation in Nigeria' [2012] Economic Insights, Trends and Challenges, LXIV 1 1-8.

[104] Section 5(1)(a).

[105] Section 5(1)(b). This would represent a major step in order to overcome the already noted mainstream scheme which is possible to observe in the investment contracts between MNCs and Nigeria.

The same Section, however, also mentions the compliance to the WTO rules. It is doubtful, therefore, whether this Section will actually be able to allow the country to include enforceable environmental requirements in the investment contracts, and, most of all, whether these requirements would prevail over free trade provisions.

responsibility for a given year should not be less than 3.5% of its gross annual profit for that year.

## 3. 2. Participation and empowerment of local communities

It is reasonably arguable that, praiseworthy although its efforts are, the CSR Bill does not seem perfectly equipped for the achievement of stronger participation and empowerment of host communities. The reason lies outside the Bill itself, and it is identifiable in the combined provisions of the already mentioned LUA and CAMA.

Hence, the inclusion of an amendment to the two recalled Acts in the CSR Bill (or in any other legal instrument) is recommendable, since only such an amendment would be able to lead to a higher local people's participation in the oil development.

As regards the LUA, the vestment of all rights to the land in the federal government prevents the community involvement. As regards the CAMA, the disclosure requirements provisions should be amended, so that the access to corporations' documents would be awarded also to external stakeholders.

*3.2.1. Participation in the permit-awarding and law-making processes: indigenisation for the people*

Moreover, the CAMA could achieve its presumed goal, consisting in the indigenisation of the industrial activities in Nigeria, if the requirement of incorporation within the country was replaced (or backed up) by an indigenisation pursued for the people. In other words, instead of (or beside) basing indigenisation on grounds of incorporation, this goal should rather be pursued through the inclusion of clauses providing for the awarding of permits to run oil activities, on the grounds of MNCs' best practices. The evaluation of the corporate practices would be conducted, first of all, at the local level, and NGOs would play an important role in this regard.

This would allow to create a more fertile and dynamic public opinion and social fabric, which, in turn, would represent the pillars for the implementation of the so-called Multi-Stakeholder Initiatives (MSIs).

The World Bank promotes these initiatives and recognises that they contribute to "level the playing field [inasmuch as they allow the] weaker stakeholders [to] have an opportunity to look more powerful stakeholders in the eye and to persuade them of their positions."[106]

However, local host communities should not only have the first say in the decision about the feasibility of single oil development projects, but also be empowered of the right to give their essential imprinting in the law-making process, that – as a result – would be fairer and more inclusive: this, in turn, would generate an environment in which different actors cooperate for the better.[107]

---

[106] Colland, 'The political economy of multi-stakeholder initiatives' (worldbank.org 2014). Available at: <http://blogs.worldbank.org/governance/node/973> accessed on 14 August 2014.
Moreover, according to Roberts, MSIs represent a tool for the "dialogue across the corporate boundary with those most vulnerable to the effects of corporate conduct." See: J Roberts, 'The Manufacture of Corporate Social Responsibility: Constructing Corporate Sensibility' [2003] Organization 10:2 249.
[107] See, among others, B U Ihugba, 'The governance of corporate social responsibility: developing an inclusive regulation framework' [2014] IJLM 56 2, 105-120, and
C Nwapi, supra note 45.

## 3.3. Concluding remarks

As recognised by the United Nations:

> "The exploitation of high-value natural resources, including oil [and] gas [...] has often been cited as a key factor in triggering, escalating or sustaining violent conflicts around the globe."[108]

The UNEP has openly expressed the need for the establishment of an Environmental Restoration Fund for Ogoniland, "with an initial capital injection of US $1 billion contributed by the oil industry and the Government."[109]

Nonetheless, it is questionable whether such measure "would [...] encourage better social responsibility [...]"[110] or only represent a discharge of responsibilities for the government.

It is here found that a balanced combination of the government's and MNCs' roles would allow the local communities to implement an oil development which is sustainable and, as such, not prone to conflict.

Pertaining to this, it is a contention of this study that there is a need for the shift in the paradigm of the state regulation in this field: willingness to regulate the oil

---

[108] UN Interagency Framework Team for Preventive Action, supra note 101.
This aspect is underlined by Amnesty International: "Oil companies have been exploiting Nigeria's weak regulatory system for too long" and this has brought to "impoverishment, conflict, human rights abuses and despair to the majority of the people in the oil-producing areas". See: Amnesty International, 'Oil industry has brought poverty and pollution to Niger Delta' (Amnesty International 2009). Available at: <http://www.amnesty.org/en/news-and-updates/news/oil-industry-has-brought-poverty-and-pollution-to-niger-delta-20090630 > accessed on 14 August 2014.
In addition, as concerns the aspect of forced migration, analysed earlier in this study, Percival and Homer-Dixon – analysing the case of South Africa which could be also applied also to Nigeria – state that: "Strong community institutions are crucial for managing the social conflicts that inevitably arise from large numbers of migrants." See: V Percival and T Homer-Dixon, 'Environmental Scarcity and Violent Conflict: The Case of South Africa', JPR, 35:3. 279, 298, and
P Donnelly Roark, 'Using Participation and Empowerment to Create a Human Rights Perspective on the Environment in Africa' [1993] AUJIP 121.
[109] Supra note 63, p. 15.
[110] Okoye, supra note 103, p. 365.

industry has to be built and, as such, it is reasonable to recommend that corporations abide by international standards and best practice requirements even without a dedicated domestic law provision.[III]

---

[III] This statement has to be read alongside the previous observations regarding the role of states in the regulation of MNCs activities. This clarification is necessary in order not to empower MNCs beyond the scope of their responsibility: the role of companies should not be confused nor compared to the governments' one.

# 4. The Corporate Social (shared) Responsibility

Furthering the discussion above, it is possible to summarise a possible avenue for the resolution of the environmental and social problems, arising from oil operations in Nigeria, through a three-step scheme, in which the main involved actors would share part of the responsibility to remedy to the current situation.

This chapter will draw such a scheme.

## 4. 1. The government's responsibility

As emerges from this research and from the literature,[112] the main responsibility lies in the hands of the Nigerian federal government: it is entitled of international legal personality, as well as the institution supposed to protect the citizens and work for their development.

Hence, a stronger regulation of oil MNCs' activities in Nigeria is recommendable, inasmuch as it can place them under the obligation to abide by their own codes of conduct, not to mention the dedicated instruments in international law: as a result, using its power of sovereignty would represent a major forward step,

---

[112] The World Bank, apart from praising the MSIs' values, also clarifies that: "[while] transferring responsibilities to the local level is critical, support is still needed in terms of building capacity and facilitating process of change." See: Martinsson, 'Multistakeholder Initiatives: Are they Effective?' (worldbank.org 2011). Available at: <http://blogs.worldbank.org/publicsphere/node/5620> accessed on 14 August 2014.
Okoye highlights that "it is important, that where governments begin to engage with CSR and drive CSR developmental objectives, this must happen *alongside* action on its own responsibility for developmental objectives." (Emphasis added). See: A Okoye, supra note 103, p. 371.
The increasingly important role of governments in regulating CSR – and, by doing so, making voluntary guidelines become mandatory and enforceable legal requirements – is also recognised by Eyre. The author, nonetheless, mentions the opinions of Mr. Marc Benioff and Mr. Martin Le Jeune (head of saleforce.com and MNCs consultant, respectively), who argue that state regulation is counterproductive in this field, thus standing against compulsory regulation of CSR. See: B Eyre, 'The crusade for CSR', [2004] CL 42 20-24.

for the Nigerian national government, towards a sustainable oil development, and for the involvement of oil MNCs in such move.

As recognised by Nakajima, however, "the more intervention that the state exercises in corporate activities, the more room that exists for abuse by the state, leading to corruption."[113]

In 2004, the Nigeria Extractive Industry Transparency Initiative (NEITI) was launched in order to seek to remedy to the pervasive corruption in the Nigerian extractive industry sector.[114] Among its goals, the empowerment of the citizens by means of access to "information and data to hold government and extractive industry companies accountable"[115] is remarkable, since, as noted earlier, one of the main loopholes identifiable in the self-regulation scheme is exactly the lack of public participation in the review of the abidance by such scheme by the companies. As

---

[113] C Nakajima, 'The importance of legally embedding corporate social responsibility', [2011] CL32(9), 257-259.
The Nigerian corruption scenario is well described by O N Ogbu, 'Combating Corruption in Nigeria; A Critical Appraisal of the Laws, Institutions and Political Will' [2008] ASICL14 99.
This is a scenario which has to be avoided in the Nigerian context, already characterised by one of the highest levels of corruption in the world. Amongst the various forms of corruption in Nigeria, Ogbu lists the following: "buying of votes, election rigging and malpractices, the use of money to sway the national and state assemblies, the political donations by private corporations." Ibid., p. 259.
According to Transparency International, Nigeria is ranked 144th out of 177 surveyed countries as concerns the Corruption Perception Index. The Global Corruption Barometer, moreover, reported that in 2010 bribes in Nigeria were paid for the 63% of transactions/administrative services. See: Transparency International, 'Corruption by Country/Territory, Nigeria' (transparency.org 2014). Available at: <http://www.transparency.org/country#NGA_DataResearch> and <http://www.transparency.org/country#NGA_PublicOpinion> both accessed on 2 August 2014.
[114] The main goals of the NEITI are to "ensure due process, transparency and accountability in the payment made by extractive industry companies; [...] in the revenue receipts of the Federal Government from extractive industry companies; [...] in the prudent management of the revenue accruing from oil, gas and mining payments; [and to] ensure that all payments due to the Federal Government from extractive industry companies including taxes, royalties, dividends, penalties, levies are duly paid." See: NEITI, 'The Secretariat' (neiti.org.ng 2014). Available at: <http://neiti.org.ng/index.php?q=pages/secretariat> accessed on 2 August 2014.
[115] Ibid.

acknowledged by the NEITI itself, indeed, such empowerment would "strengthen participatory democracy."[116]

It is here contended that, while the Nigerian government must undoubtedly further this initiative, a comprehensive reconsideration of the analysed legislative framework in the oil sector is still much needed, since only such a revision and the consequent amendments, can orient the country's oil industry towards the sustainable development direction.

Alongside this, Nigeria should rapidly move to the transposition of international law instruments in the field of environment and human rights into national law.

## 4. 2. The oil MNCs' responsibility

If the role of the government is undeniably overwhelming in this field, oil MNCs have a big share in the responsibility of fixing the environmental and social damage that they contributed to generate with their activities.

Indeed, their role could be regarded as majorly important, since, if they embrace the shift from a totally market-based business model to a socially responsible one, not only they can do good for the society and environment in which they operate, but also they can benefit from such change.

In 2004, the then World Bank President, Paul Wolfowitz, recognised that:

> "[...] [In] many countries [...] regulatory frameworks are often outdated, inefficient, frequently they seem to be unchanged since colonial times. [...] There is an urgent need for [...] solutions that link entrepreneurship and competitiveness with respect for social and environmental norms.

---

[116] Ibid.

[...] It's a collaboration that is in the *self-interest of business* and in the best interest of the poor living in developing countries." [117] (Emphasis added).

These statements show that MNCs have become aware of the possible benefits they can receive from a socially responsible way of doing business.

Nonetheless, this work recommends a further step: MNCs should abandon the pattern followed so far, which consists in modelling their business conducts according to the situation of the country where they operate. Of course, especially in the African context, companies have to bear in mind the peculiarities of different nations and communities. Precisely for this reason, the adoption of double standards in managing pollution and waste, not to mention the strategy of avoiding negotiation and mediation in order to stop the affected communities from suing them, must be abandoned.

Therefore, as already stressed in paragraph 3.2.2., oil MNCs operating in the Niger Delta should abide by international standards even in the absence of their transposition into national law. By doing so, they would work in a better environment, meanwhile creating an incentive for the government to comply with the international standards.

People's interests are currently excluded from the mutual exchange between government and oil MNCs: this is the reason of local discontent. Ukeje describes the

---

[117] See: World Bank, 'Corporate Social Responsibility: Good for Business, Remarks to Business for Social Responsibility Conference, Washington, DC' (web.worldbank.org 2005). Available at: <http://web.worldbank.org/WBSITE/EXTERNAL/NEWS/0,,contentMDK:21195595~pagePK:64257 043~piPK:437376~theSitePK:4607,00.html> accessed on1 August 2014.
A further confirm to the utmost importance of the MNCs' role in achieving CSR good practices, comes from the Unilever CEO, Niall Fitzgerald; see: Elliott, 'Cleaning Agent. Interview: Niall FitzGerald, co-chairman and chief executive, Unilever' (theguardian.com 2003). Available at: <http://www.theguardian.com/business/2003/jul/05/unilever1#> accessed on 2 August 2014.

complicity between these two actors in sharing the benefits of oil profits and revenues without involving local people, rather harmfully affecting them. The author highlights that:

> "[Oil] companies have become *the 'government' that the communities see and relate to on a daily basis*. [...] The cumulative effect of state repression is that protests have turned violent, amid increased hostility towards multinational oil companies making it very difficult for them to engage in oil [...] activities without elaborate security protection from the state.[118] (Emphasis added)."

The above-described recommendation, therefore, would serve as a tool to reverse this vicious circle.

## 4. 3. The communities' responsibility

The Nigerian communities are called to work for their own sustainable development by abandoning the violent strategy and focusing on the existent available avenues.

The decision in the *Gbemre v Shell*[119] case has maintained that the gas flaring practice was in violation of the right to a clean environment, sanctioned in the ACHPR. The Economic Community of West African States (ECOWAS) Treaty, moreover, urges the member states to recognise, promote and protect human rights according to the African Charter.[120]

---

[118] C Ukeje, 'Changing the paradigm of pacification: oil and militarization in Niger Delta's Region' in C Obi and S A Rustad (eds), *Oil and insurgency in the Niger Delta, Managing the complex politics of petro-violence* (1st, Zed Books Ltd., Uppsala, Sweden 2011), 94.
[119] *Gbemre v Shell Petroleum Development Company Nigeria Limited and Others* [2005] AHRLR 151 (NgHC 2005).
[120] The ECOWAS Treaty is available at: <http://ries.
www.comm.ecowas.int/sec/?id=treaty&lang=en> accessed on 2 August 2014.

Thus, case law shows that Nigerian courts have embraced the regional human rights and environmental protection framework, even without a well-framed national legal scheme to implement them.

In pursuing the goal of reaffirmation of their rights, the Nigerian communities would have to rely upon the various NGOs operating in the Niger Delta, which can provide technical and legal expertise to the plaintiffs.

However, overstressing the importance of NGOs would turn to be an obstacle to the development of an indigenous legal and technical capability in these communities. As a result, in order to achieve a self-determined sustainable development through the actual community-based ownership and management of oil, support must be given to the "development of local capacity [...]."[121]

The OECD Guidelines for Multinational Enterprises incentivise the "mutual confidence between enterprises and the societies in which they operate"[122], as well as their "contribution to sustainable development".[123] In 2008, however – as reported by German Watch – various civil society groups from a number of African countries, amongst which Nigeria, engaged in a seminar on the effectiveness of the Guidelines in the view of holding multinational businesses accountable for human rights violations and socio-environmental damages. In this context, one of the main

---

[121] U J Orji, 'Towards sustainable local content development in the Nigerian oil and gas industry: an appraisal of the legal framework and challenges – Part 1' IELR [2004] 1, 30-42.
This is the objective of the Oil and Gas Industry Content Development Act – a goal that has not been achieved yet.
Here, Orji considerably disagree with Ako, who stresses the importance of relying on NGOs for technical and legal consulting. See: R Ako, 'The struggle for resource control and violence in the Niger Delta' in C Obi and S A Rustad (eds), *Oil and insurgency in the Niger Delta, Managing the complex politics of petro-violence* (1st, Zed Books Ltd., Uppsala, Sweden 2011) 54
[122] Organisation for Economic Co-operation and Development, 'Guidelines for Multinational Enterprises' (oecd.org 2011), p. 13. Available at: <http://www.oecd.org/daf/inv/mne/48004323.pdf> accessed on 15 August 2014.
[123] Ibid.

recommendations of the seminar consisted in the call for the raising of awareness and the strengthening of governments and civil society in host countries.[124]

Two crucial elements for the empowerment and capacity-building of Nigerian people are, firstly, a stronger priority awarded to the domestic products manufacture, linked to a better integration among different economic sectors and a higher diversification of the economy, and, secondly, a higher attention to the local academic institutions, which can develop an indigenous technical and legal knowledge.[125]

## 4. 4. Concluding Remarks

Government and oil MNCs ought to stop working for their exclusive advantage and take into consideration the people's needs and claims: by embracing the sustainability concepts in oil development, they would avoid discontent and conflict. The community approach to development should be given the opportunity to guide the exploitation of natural resources and to manage the challenges arising from it.[126] For their part, local communities should push for the reaffirmation of their rights and for the protection of their environment in a non-violent way, demonstrating their willingness to stop the conflict in order to halt the companies from claiming that their good practices are impeded by the endemic violence in the region.

The slow – if not absent – amendment process to the national provisions in the field of oil and – more broadly, in the regulation of MNCs – and, on the other hand,

---

[124] See: GermanWatch, 'OECD Guidelines for Multinational Enterprises must be improved' (germanwatch.org 2008). Available at: < http://germanwatch.org/corp/camsem08.pdf> accessed on 15 August 2014.
[125] Ibid.
[126] K S A Ebeku, supra note 9, 156.

the lack of a prompt transposition of international human rights and environment protection instruments into national law, combined with the corrupt and conflicting Nigerian situation, produce a stalemate in the process towards a sustainable oil development in the country. The steps recommended by this study constitute a possible suitable avenue to overcome this stalemate: it will be the scope of further research to explore the feasibility of the suggested pattern in the country.

As already seen, however, the case law and the opinions of reputable international institutions and authors show that the review of the mainstream corporate practices, implemented so far by oil multinationals in the Niger Delta, is much needed, and that local people should be allowed to access justice through the existent regional legal framework.

The increased remedy effort by the oil multinationals will not express its full potential if not backed up by the amendment of the Nigerian legal framework; similarly, local communities will not be able to entirely reaffirm their social, economic, and environmental rights if the state will not implement the international instruments dedicated to the protection of such rights.

# Bibliography

## CASES

- *Akpan v Royal Dutch Shell Plc* [2013] No. 337050/HA ZA 09-1580 (District Court of the Hague).
- *Gbemre v Shell Petroleum Development Company Nigeria Limited and Others* [2005] AHRLR 151 (NgHC 2005).
- *Social and Economic Rights Action Centre (SERAC) and Another v Nigeria* [2001] AHRLR 60 (ACHPR 2001).
- *Wiwa v. Royal Dutch Petroleum Co.* [2001] 226 F.3d 88 (2d Cir. 2000), 532 U.S. 941.

## NIGERIAN NATIONAL LEGISLATIONS

- Companies and Allied Matters Act 1990.
- Constitution of the Federal Republic of Nigeria.
- CSR Bill 2008.
- Land Use Act 1978.
- National Environmental Standards and Regulations Enforcement Agency (Establishment) Act 2007.
- National Oil Spill Detection and Response Agency Act 2006.
- Niger Delta Development Commission (Establishment etc.) Act 2000.
- Oil Pipelines Act 1956.
- Petroleum (Drilling and Production) Regulations 1969.
- Petroleum Act 1969.
- Petroleum Industry Bill 2012.

## INTERNATIONAL CONVENTIONS

- African Charter on Human and Peoples' Rights 1981.
- Convention Against Torture and Other Cruel, Inhuman or Degrading Treatment or Punishment 1984.
- Economic Community of West African Countries 1975.
- International Convention on Oil Pollution Preparedness, Response and Co-operation 1990.
- International Covenant on Civil and Political Rights 1966.
- International Covenant on Economic, Social, and Cultural Rights 1966.

- United Nation Declaration on the Rights of Indigenous People, adopted by Resolution of the General Assembly No. 61/295.
- United Nations Draft Norms on the Responsibilities of Transnational Corporations and Other Business Enterprises with Regard to Human Rights, E/CN.4/Sub.2/2003/12 (2003)


## JOURNAL ARTICLES

- Adewale, O 'Oil Spill Compensation Claims in Nigeria: Principles, Guidelines and Criteria' [1989] JAL, 33, 91-104.
- Adomokai, R Sheate, W R 'Community participation and environmental decision-making in the Niger Delta' [2004] EIAR 24 495-518.
- Ako, R 'Nigeria's Land Use Act: an anti-thesis to environmental justice' [2009] JAL 53:2, 293.
- Amao, O O 'Corporate Social Responsibility, Multinational Corporations and the Law in Nigeria: Controlling Multinationals in Host States' [2008] JAL 52 89-113.
- Atsegbua, L 'Environmental rights, pipeline vandalisation and conflict resolution in Nigeria', [2001] IELTR, 5, 89-92.
- Donnelly Roark, P 'Using Participation and Empowerment to Create a Human Rights Perspective on the Environment in Africa' [1993] AUJIP 121.
- Ebeku, K S A 'Compensation for damage arising from oil operations: Shell Petroleum Development Company of Nigeria v Ambah revisited' [2002] IELTR 155, 156.
- Egede, E 'Bringing human rights home: an examination of the domestication of human rights treaties in Nigeria' [2007] JAL 249, 265.
- Ejims, O 'The impact of Nigerian international petroleum contracts on environmental and human rights of indigenous communities' [2013] AJICL 345, 349.
- Emeseh E et al., Corporations, CSR and Self Regulation: What Lessons from the Global Financial Crisis? GLJ [2010] 11, 2, 230-259.
- Eyre, B 'The crusade for CSR', [2004] CL 42 20-24.
- Graham, D and Woods, N 'Making Corporate Self-Regulation Effective in Developing Countries' [2006] World Development 34:5, 868–883.
- Idowu, A A 'Human Rights, Environmental Degradation and Oil Multinational Companies in Nigeria: the Ogoniland Episode', [1999] 17 Neth. Q. Hum. Rts. 161.
- Ihugba, B U 'The governance of corporate social responsibility: developing an inclusive regulation framework' [2014] IJLM 56 2, 105-120.
- Le Billon, P 'Oil and Armed Conflict in Africa' [2012] Afr. Geo. Rev. 29 1 63, 81.
- McConnell, L J 'Establishing liability for multinational oil companies in parent/subsidiary relationships' [2014] ELR 50, 51.
- Mordi, C Opoyemi, I S Tonbara, M Ojo, S 'Corporate Social Responsibility and the Legal Regulation in Nigeria' [2012] Economic Insights, Trends and

Challenges, LXIV 1 1-8.

- Muchlinkski, P T 'Human rights and multinationals: is there a problem?' [2001] International Affairs 77 1 31 – 48.
- Nakajima, C 'The importance of legally embedding corporate social responsibility', [2011] CL32(9), 257-259.
- Ntongho, R 'Self-regulation of corporate governance in Africa: following the bandwagon?' ICCLR [2009] 20(2), 427-435.
- Nwapi, C 'A legislative proposal for public participation in oil and gas decision-making in Nigeria' [2010] JAL 184, 187.
- Ogbu, O N 'Combating Corruption in Nigeria; A Critical Appraisal of the Laws, Institutions and Political Will' [2008] ASICL14 99.
- Ogutuga, M 'CSR obligations of Transnational Corporations and legal enforcement mechanisms in extractive industries: how effective are these mechanisms in the protection of Human Rights in Africa?' [2009] CELMPM Annual Review, Vol.13.
- Ojukwu-Ogba, N E 'Legislating development in Nigeria's oil producing region: the NDDC Act sever years on' [2009] AJICL 136, 137.
- Okoye, A 'Exploring the relationship between corporate social responsibility, law and development in an African context: should government be responsible for ensuring corporate responsibility?' [2012] IJLM.
- Opukri, C O and Ibaba, I S 'Oil induced environmental degradation and internal population displacement in the Niger Delta' [e.g. 2005] JSDA 185, 188.
- Orji, U J 'Towards sustainable local content development in the Nigerian oil and gas industry: an appraisal of the legal framework and challenges – Part 1' IELR [2004] 1, 30-42.
- Osa Ekhator, E 'Environmental Protection in the oil and gas industry in Nigeria: the roles of governmental agencies' [2013] IELR 196, 203.
- Oshionebo, E 'Transnational corporations, civil society organisations and social accountability in Nigeria's oil and gas industry' [2007] AJICL 107, 108.
- Panter-Brick, S K 'The Right to Self-determination: its application to Nigeria' [1968] International Affairs (Royal Institute of International Affairs 1944) 44 2 254-266.
- Percival, V and Homer-Dixon, T 'Environmental Scarcity and Violent Conflict: The Case of South Africa', JPR, 35:3. 279, 298.
- Richardson, B J 'Socially Responsible Investing for Sustainability: Overcoming Its Incomplete and Conflicting Rationales', [2013] TEL 2:2 311-338.
- Roberts, J 'The Manufacture of Corporate Social Responsibility: Constructing Corporate Sensibility' [2003] Organization 10:2 249.

*BOOKS*

- Frynas, J G *Oil in Nigeria, Conflict and Litigation between Oil Companies and Village Communities*. LIT, London 2000.
- Villiers, C *Corporate Reporting and Company Law* (1st, Cambridge University Press, e.g. Oxford 2006).
- Maass, P *Crude World, The violent twilight of oil* (1st, Alfred A. Knopf, New York 2009).
- Muchlinski, P T *Multinational Enterprises and the Law* (2nd Edition). OUP, Oxford 2007.
- Obi, C and Rustad, S A *Oil and Insurgency in the Niger Delta, Managing the complex politics of petro-violence* (1st, Zed Books Ltd., Uppsala, Sweden 2011).
- Oshionebo, E *Regulating transnational corporations in domestic and international regimes an African case study*, University of Toronto Press Inc., Toronto 2009.


*ONLINE SOURCES*

- A I Osuoka, 'Oil and Gas Revenues and Development Challenges for the Niger Delta in Nigeria, Expert Group Meeting on the Use of Non-Renewable Energy Resource Revenues for Sustainable Local Development' (un.org 2007). Available at: <http://www.un.org/esa/sustdev/sdissues/institutional_arrangements/egm2007/presentations/isaacOsuoka.pdf>
  - Ahmed, 'Behind the rise of Boko Haram - ecological disaster, oil crisis, spy games Islamist militancy in Nigeria is being strengthened by western and regional fossil fuel interests' (theguardian.com last update 2014). Available at: <http://www.theguardian.com/environment/earth-insight/2014/may/09/behind-rise-nigeria-boko-haram-climate-disaster-peak-oil-depletion>
- Amnesty International, 'Oil industry has brought poverty and pollution to Niger Delta' (Amnesty International 2009). Available at: <http://www.amnesty.org/en/news-and-updates/news/oil-industry-has-brought-poverty-and-pollution-to-niger-delta-20090630 >
- Amnesty International, 'Nigeria: Petroleum, Pollution and Poverty in the Niger Delta' (amnesty.org 2009). Available at: <http://www.amnesty.org/en/library/asset/AFR44/017/2009/en/e2415061-da5c-44f8-a73c-a7a4766ee21d/afr440172009en.pdf>
- Apata, 'Linkages between Crude-oil Exploration and Agricultural Development in Nigeria: Implications for relevant qualitative data collection and analysis to improve rural economy.' (fao.org 2010) <http://www.fao.org/fileadmin/templates/ess/pages/rural/wye_city_group/2010/May/WYE_2010.4.3_Apata.pdf>
- Benner and Witte, 'Rules for Global Players? Governing multinational corporations in developing countries'. (gppi.net 2006). Available at: <http://www.gppi.net/fileadmin/gppi/IP_Benner-Whitte.pdf>

- Business Council for Sustainable Energy, 'Sustainable energy in America. Factbook 2014' (bcse.org 2014). Available at:
- <http://www.bcse.org/factbook/pdfs/2014%20Sustainable%20Energy%20in%20 America%20Factbook.pdf>
- Chevron, 'Business Conduct and Ethics Code' (chevron.com 2014). Available at: <http://www.chevron.com/documents/pdf/chevronbusinessconductethicscode. pdf> both accessed on 30 July 2014.
- CIA, 'The World Fact-book Nigeria' (cia.gov 2014). Available at: <https://www.cia.gov/library/publications/the-world-factbook/geos/ni.html>
- Colland, 'The political economy of multi-stakeholder initiatives' (worldbank.org 2014). Available at: <http://blogs.worldbank.org/governance/node/973>
- Elliott, 'Cleaning Agent. Interview: Niall FitzGerald, co-chairman and chief executive, Unilever' (theguardian.com 2003). Available at: <http://www.theguardian.com/business/2003/jul/05/unilever1#> accessed on 2 August 2014.
- European Commission, 'Sustainable, secure and affordable energy for Europeans' (europa.eu 2013). Available at: <http://europa.eu/pol/ener/flipbook/en/files/energy.pdf>
- Federal Environment Protection Agency, 'National Policy on the Environment' (nesrea.org 1998). Available at: <http://www.nesrea.org/images/National%20Policy%20on%20Environment.pd f>
- GermanWatch, 'OECD Guidelines for Multinational Enterprises must be improved' (germanwatch.org 2008). Available at: < http://germanwatch.org/corp/camsem08.pdf>
- Human Rights Watch, 'Nigeria: UPR Submission March 2013' (hrw.org 2013). Available at: <http://www.hrw.org/news/2013/10/17/nigeria-upr-submission-march-2013>
- Human Rights Watch, 'The Price of Oil. Corporate Social Responsibility and Human Rights Violations in Nigeria's Oil Producing Communities.' (hrw.org 1999). Available at: <http://www.hrw.org/reports/1999/nigeria/nigeria0199.pdf>
- Human Rights Watch, 'The Warri Crisis, Fueling Violence' (hrw.org 2003). Available at: <http://www.hrw.org/node/12203/section/2>
- Martinsson, 'Multistakeholder Initiatives: Are they Effective?' (worldbank.org 2011). Available at: <http://blogs.worldbank.org/publicsphere/node/5620>
- National Emergency Management Agency, '16,470 Persons still in IDP camps' (nema.gov 2014). Available at: <http://nema.gov.ng/16470-displaced-persons-still-in-idp-camps/>
- NEITI, 'The Secretariat' (neiti.org.ng 2014). Available at: <http://neiti.org.ng/index.php?q=pages/secretariat>
- Nyheim, Zandviliet, Morissey, 'Peace and Security in the Niger Delta: Conflict Expert Group Baseline Report,' (npr 2003) Available at: <http://www.npr.org/documents/2005/aug/shell_wac_report.pdf>
- Organisation for Economic Co-operation and Development, 'Guidelines for Multinational Enterprises' (oecd.org 2011), p. 13. Available at:

<http://www.oecd.org/daf/inv/mne/48004323.pdf>
- Ploch, 'Nigeria: Current Issues and U.S. Policy' (Federation of American Scientists 2012), 13. Available at: <http://fas.org/sgp/crs/row/RL33964.pdf>
- Raidt and Smith, 'Advancing U.S., African, and Global Interests: Security and Stability in the West African Maritime Domain' (atlanticcouncil.org 2010). Available at: <http://www.atlanticcouncil.org/images/files/publication_pdfs/3/advancing-us-african-global-interests-security-stability-west-africa-maritime-domain.pdf>
- Sayne, Mahdavi, Heller, Schreuder, 'The Petroleum Industry Bill and the Future of NNPC' (RevenueWatch.org 2012) available at: <http://www.revenuewatch.org/publications/petroleum-industry-bill-and-future-nnpc>
- Sende, 'The Responsibilities of States for Actions of Transnational Corporations Affecting Social and Economic Rights: A Comparative Analysis of the Duty to Protect' (cjel.net 2009). Available at: <http://www.cjel.net/online/15_2-marsella-sende/>
- Shell, 'Code of Conduct' (shell.com 2010). Available at: <http://www.shell.com/global/aboutshell/who-we-are/our-values/code-of-conduct.html>
- Shell, 'Politically sensitive regions' (shell.com). Available at: <http://www.shell.com/global/environment-society/society/business/politically-sensitive-regions.html>
- The Business Council for Sustainable Energy, 'Sustainable energy in America. Fact-book 2014' (bcse.org 2014). Available at:
- <http://www.bcse.org/factbook/pdfs/2014%20Sustainable%20Energy%20in%20America%20Factbook.pdf>
- Transparency International, 'Corruption by Country/Territory, Nigeria' (transparency.org 2014). Available at: <http://www.transparency.org/country#NGA_DataResearch>
- UN General Assembly, 'General Assembly adopts Declaration on Rights of Indigenous Peoples' (un.org 2007). Available at: <http://www.un.org/News/Press/docs/2007/ga10612.doc.htm>
- UN Global Compact, 'Global Corporate Sustainability Report' (unglobalcompact.org 2013). Available at: <http://www.unglobalcompact.org/docs/about_the_gc/Global_Corporate_Sustainability_Report2013.pdf>
- UN Interagency Framework Team for Preventive Action, 'Renewable Resources and Conflict. Toolkit and Guidance for Managing Land and Natural Resources Conflict' (un.org 2012). Available at: <http://www.un.org/en/events/environmentconflictday/pdf/GN_Renewable_Consultation.pdf>
- UNHCR, 'Global Estimates 2011, People displaced by natural hazard-induced disasters' (unhcr.org 2011). Available at: <http://www.unhcr.org/50f95fcb9.html>
- UNHCR, 'Internally Displaced People, On the run in their own land' (unhcr.org 2014). Available at:

&lt;http://www.unhcr.org/pages/49c3646c146.html&gt;
- United Nations Environment Programme, 'Environmental Assessment of Ogoniland' (unep.org 2011). Available at: &lt;http://postconflict.unep.ch/publications/OEA/UNEP_OEA.pdf&gt;
- Universitat Pompeu Fabra Barcelona, 'Nigeria: Issues and dilemmas' (econ.epf.edu 2004). Available at: &lt;http://www.econ.upf.edu/~lemenestrel/IMG/pdf/shell_nigeria_website-2.pdf&gt;
- University of Minnesota. Human Rights Library, 'Ratification of International Human Rights Treaties - Nigeria' (umn.edu 2012 – last update). Available at: &lt;http://www1.umn.edu/humanrts/research/ratification-nigeria.html&gt;
- Utting, 'Rethinking Business Regulation. From Self-Regulation to Social Control' (unrisd.org 2005), p. 1. Available at: &lt;http://www.unrisd.org/80256B3C005BCCF9/(httpAuxPages)/F02AC3DB0ED406E0C12570A10029BEC8/$file/utting.pdf&gt;
- World Bank, 'Corporate Social Responsibility: Good for Business, Remarks to Business for Social Responsibility Conference, Washington, DC. ' (web.worldbank.org 2005). Available at: &lt;http://web.worldbank.org/WBSITE/EXTERNAL/NEWS/0,,contentMDK:21195595~pagePK:64257043~piPK:437376~theSitePK:4607,00.html&gt;
- World Bank, 'Corporate Social Responsibility: Good for Business, Remarks to Business for Social Responsibility Conference, Washington, DC' (web.worldbank.org 2005). Available at: &lt;http://web.worldbank.org/WBSITE/EXTERNAL/NEWS/0,,contentMDK:21195595~pagePK:64257043~piPK:437376~theSitePK:4607,00.html

- *Acknowledgments*

I shall express my gratitude to the Division of Law and Philosophy, University of Stirling, for giving me the opportunity to carry out this research, in such a controversial topic as the socio-environmental consequences of the oil industry in Nigeria.

Many thanks to Dr. Raphael Heffron, for his precious academic and human support, and for Making the Most of Me.

Special thanks to Ilary and to all my friends: in particular, Lorenzo and Eva, Matteo and Francesca, Sandra, Andrei, Mohamed, Dom and Erminia: I know you believed in me.

Last but definitely not the least, thanks to Angelo and Antonella, my never-ending, huge and simple inspirations.

# About the author

Roberto Cui was born in Iglesias, Italy, in 1987.

After a bachelor degree in Political Sciences and a Master Degree in International Relations at the University of Cagliari, he obtained a Master of Law Degree in International Energy Law and Policy at the University of Stirling, Scotland.

His research interests consist in the analysis of international dynamics as concerns the relationship between big powers and developing countries. In particular, he stresses the importance of energy in defining the global and regional assets of power. In this regard, he has specialised in the study of the oil Multinational enterprises' interference in the human rights performance of least developed, resource-rich countries. Moreover, his study method is characterised by a constant quest for the avenues through which such countries can possibly amend their legal structure and achieve a sustainable energy resources development.